CYNTHOLOGY

A **COLLECTION** OF **RHYMES**
BOOK II - ELECTRIFIED

CYNTHIA YOUNG

authorHOUSE®

AuthorHouse™
1663 Liberty Drive
Bloomington, IN 47403
www.authorhouse.com
Phone: 1 (800) 839-8640

This is a work of fiction. All of the characters, names, incidents, organizations, and dialogue in this novel are either the products of the author's imagination or are used fictitiously.

Published by AuthorHouse 04/09/2015

ISBN: 978-1-5049-0468-1 (sc)
ISBN: 978-1-5049-0467-4 (e)

Library of Congress Control Number: 2015905106

Print information available on the last page.

This book is printed on acid-free paper.

First paperback edition

For information about special discounts for bulk purchases, please contact Cynthia Young, at www.cyoungbooks.com

Available in E-Book and Soft Copy at www.authorhouse.com

Cover design by Shutterstock©

Contents

Cynthology A Collection Of Rhymes

Introduction

I have been a caregiver since 2002. I wrote **Memoirs of a Caregiver** to tell my story. While I was writing this book, I felt the weight of many years of love, tears, frustration and grief. I wrote my first rhyme for my aunt's funeral service. After that, it seemed as though they were always in my head. Writing them down became a much needed diversion from everything else I had going on and it became my escape. I finally decided to publish them as **Cynthology A Collection of Rhymes** which depicted my view on life.

I was inspired by my readers' to write a second book of (unedited) rhymes after my first book was so well received. **Cynthology A Collection of Rhymes Book II – Electrified** is a compilation of more original rhymes and the most popular readers' favorites from my first collection.

Readers' of the first book ranged from eighteen to eighty and were touched by the rhymes on subjects they were familiar with and could relate to. **Book II – Electrified** also has rhymes that speak to past and modern day issues and common situations that people deal with frequently. These rhymes are not *nursery school* rhymes and depict mature subject matter for the grown and sexy.

They tell stories that may leave you with a message to ponder. I hope you find these rhymes to be thought provoking, inspirational, uplifting, even shocking. This is my version of poetry that is relatable and understandable.

Once again, please enjoy the rhymes and find your favorites from this collection too.

Enjoy!

Cynthia Young

Dedicated to those that stood with me in
the past, stand with me now
and look forward with me to the future

Cynthology

Cynthology© is my view on life
From being a kid in a good neighborhood
To becoming a wife

Life is good, bad or indifferent
I've been to the school of
Hard knocks and bumps
Believe me, I've
Paid my dues and handled my lumps

Love, happiness, loved ones loss
I dealt with many until
They went home to the big Boss

I have good friends, known many men
And stuck with the good one
That put a ring on it in the end

Now it's my time to shine
Drink some wine and dine
Drive the rode and see what
I dream about

I'm finally free to be me and I want to
Shout it out!

A Kiss

A wet and sloppy kisser drools all over you
There is nothing sexy about that kiss
It's not a hit it's a total miss

A kiss that is soft and sensual caresses your lips
Like the fresh morning dew
It warms your heart and goes deep into your soul
This kind of kiss never, ever gets old

A kiss stirs the juices that pulsate through your body
The flick of the tongue and the warm breath
On your ear, down your neck and along your arm

Heats you up from head to toe, but it's what's
Happening in the middle that makes you know
That the kiss is what really starts the show

Kisses that skim the body and make you go limp
A kiss that makes you moan softly to let
Your lover know, that his kiss has
Stoked the fires down below

The very first kiss sets the tone for whether
You want to stay or go home, get it right
It will determine the rest of your night
Kissing slow soft and tender brings the
Butterflies and the willingness to surrender

A Song

A song can tell a story so real, so true
It makes you drop your head back and
Close your eyes, to see what it is telling you

Soft and slow, fast and loud a song pleases many crowds
Behind closed doors lovers love, binding their
Bodies like a tight glove

A song makes you remember that special lover who
Took you to places during sex you had never discovered

Those memories still bring butterflies to your stomach
And chills down your spine
As you slowly sip your glass of wine, you think about
A special song that makes you feel this way every time

Age Doesn't Matter

Baby boomers are reaching their prime
Looking better in their later years than any other time
Living longer, exercising and staying stronger
Age doesn't matter it's just a number

Hairstyles banging, short dresses and high heel shoes
The boomers these days aren't singing the blues
There may be snow on the mountain, but there
Is still fire in the stove, age says one thing
But it doesn't have to say old

Achieving black belts late in age, starting a new
Career writing poems on a page
Age doesn't matter just do what you do, because
Growing old gracefully will look good on you

Hanging out, grooving and moving
Age doesn't matter when you do
What you love and your youth is at heart
Age only matters when you have trouble
Controlling your farts

Always Near

August 07, 2012
(My mom's Sunset)

Today, I feel like going for a walk
So I can talk with you. I am quiet as I listen
To all the things you tell me I should do

Gone but never far away, I feel your presence
By me every day

A little bird comes to my yard, sits on
The fence and looks at me. I know
You're watching your messages are clear

Losing you was my greatest fear
I'm not worried now because I know
You may be gone from here but you
Are always near

Apron Strings

A Mother holds her sons in high esteem each one
Of them stokes another one of her dreams

She raised them as a single Mom, their Dad
Was killed in a robbery on the other side of town
Her son's are good boys, handsome and viral

She wants the best for them and scrutinizes
All their girls and tightens her hold
There will be no baby Momma drama
In her boy's world

She is obsessed with them even when they
Are grown men, she can't cut her apron strings
To let them do their own thing

The son's know her intentions are good
But her obsession with them goes way
Beyond motherhood, they want her to
Let them go and tell her so

She listens but she does not hear, her heart is breaking
And she lives in fear that a woman will come along and
Without her blessings, they won't pick the right one

She's their Mother, she knows what is best
She can't stay out of their lives; but the
Question is this, will she run them away
And be alone for the rest of her days?

This is just the opposite of her dream
So, she'd better think again and cut
Those apron strings

Ashes

Ashes represent broken dreams, disappointments
Failures, hurts and lost loved ones

Mourning should be for a season and not a lifetime
Stop mourning over what you can not change
Forgive betrayal, let go of your questions and the blame

Stop living in the rearview mirror of life
Look through the big windshield that shows you
The way to a future that is greater than your past

The enemy loves to see you sitting in the ashes
Feeling sorry for yourself. Get up, dust those ashes off
Hold your head up high and spit in the enemies' eye

One door closes and another one opens to show
You a bigger better future and a brighter day
Look to the future and ***blow*** those ashes away

Attitude

These days, attitudes are getting, meaner
And more out of control

Young people wag their fingers in your face
Roll their necks and tell you off

This attitude would not fly back in the day
Your parents would have plenty to say –
"I brought you in this world, I'll take you out"
Was often what they would shout!

Kid, don't let your attitude and your
Smart mouth write a check your
Ass can't cash

Mothers and Fathers are fighting back
Checking that attitude right and left
Sit down, shut up and listen because
That attitude needs some serious adjusting

Cynthia Young

Bad Kitty

Bad Kitty is on the prowl, night after night
She puts on her high heels, great big hair
Puffs her nose and leaves her lair

Bad Kitty, is full of revenge, she's had her
Fill of selfish, egotistical, abusive men
The only thing on her mind now, is getting even

The last man she had wasn't cool, he sexed her
And didn't use anything to protect his tool

For her it's too late, she was too naïve
She let him touch her without a rubber sleeve
Of course he never mentioned he had a disease

Now Bad Kitty is a hot mess; she's on fire
And not in a good way, she's out for
Revenge and someone is going to pay

She's in the club and finds a new love, they
Head for bed and sex their way to a sweaty frenzy
She was successful in getting him to keep it real
She told him she liked the way *bareback* feels

No raincoat, no hat, Bad Kitty passed on
The disease that made her hot, she knows
What she did was not right
But, she'll keep sharing night after night

She's full of revenge, so look out men
Bad Kitty is looking for you, avoid her tease
And please, use a sleeve when you feel the need
Or you'll go out like Bad Kitty with a fatal disease

Be Grateful

I am so very grateful for all the blessings that have been
Bestowed upon me

Good health, dreams realized, family and friends
Standing by my side, these are the things that
Make my world complete

I've walked the peaks and valley's and come out on
The bright side, I have known incredible pain and
From that there was invaluable knowledge gained

Never take for granted anything that you have, it can
Be here today, gone tomorrow in the blink of an eye
Be grateful for your blessings until the day you die

Boss Lady

Even though you don't know her, you recognize her
When she enters a room holding her head up high and
You instinctively know, that she is the type of woman
That looks you straight in the eye

A woman that's in control, bold but never brash
A boss that commands respect, she takes on what
Needs to be done and never flinches, she is
The person you want with you in the trenches

Seeing her in action can make your head swirl, she leaves
No doubt that she is the boss of her world; knocking down
Challenges that keep on coming, any job you give her
Just know, she is the right woman

She is a Boss Lady all the way, she knows how to
Embrace her softer side as she reaches out
To those in need and takes it all in stride

Straight talk with no chaser, she says what she means and
Means what she says. A Boss Lady handles her business
With style and grace and she proves over and over again
That she earned her highly coveted place

Brass Balls

When you act like a fool and show your ass
Talking smack and being mean
You must remember that the words you speak
Can come back to haunt you; but you're
So hateful I know it won't even faze you

You've dissed me for months and showed no respect
Now out of the blue I get your text and
You're asking me to help you again
You think you can do anything to me
Just because we are kin

You've got brass balls calling me to help you out
When you've got me so jacked up I can't see my way out
Take your brass balls and keep it moving
Because you and I are not grooving

Whatever you've been doing all these months
Keep doing what you do; since you've
Been gone, I've been happy without you

I've always been in your corner and I love you to death
But, I will not put up with any more of your drama
And disrespect. I need an apology with depth
So don't contact me again until you can come correct

Busted

In the middle of the night my brother and I were sliding
Along the wall on our way down the hall

When all of a sudden we stop in our tracks at the noise we
Hear from Mommy and Daddy's room, so we tip towards
The noise coming through the crack in the door

Our mouths and eyes fly open wide at what we see and hear
Oh my, what is Daddy doing to Mommy Dear?

What is Daddy doing to her that's shaking the bed?
I'll never get these images out of my head
I've never heard Mommy say those words
Is that what you call an action verb?

Now Daddy is moaning too, maybe I should call
911 — Oh no, Daddy must be okay, he says
He's going to come right away

Pretty soon the commotion stops and the bed
No longer rocks, so my brother and I open
The door and rush right in; but Mommy and Daddy
Shoo us away and tell us to go to our rooms and play

My goodness what's the fuss, we know
What they were doing is how they got us!

Cartoons, Cowboys & Superheroes

Little girls and boys awoke early on Saturday morning
Excited to see what awaited them on TV

A bowl of cold milk and Cheerios kept
Your stomach from growling, as you watched
The Road Runner and Wiley Coyote running and howling

Bugs Bunny and Mr. Magoo had us
Mimicking, what's up Doc? 'cuz we
Thought it made us sound cool

Mickey and Minnie sang and danced
They were cute with their romance and
There was Mighty Mouse, these were
The images that filled our house

The Lone Ranger and Tonto saved the day
Superman had Lois Lane, she eventually
Found out about his phone booth game

Cheyenne, six foot six handled a gun lightning quick
Batman saved Gotham City while Tarzan flew through the jungle
Popeye the Sailor Man, Brutus and Olive Oyl also entertained you

Who can forget Roy Rogers, Dale Evans and Trigger
Preserved in their museum forever

Marshall Dillon and Miss Kitty, where the King and
Queen of Dodge City, she was red headed and
Feisty, but Dillon never made her his Wifey

These childhood memories of yesteryear are
Memories I will always hold dear
Thank goodness for re-runs that let me still
Watch them, year after year

Cynthia Young

Chasing Dreams

Young and free with so many things to do and see
Take your time and explore the world
Youth is fleeting, there will be plenty
Of time to settle down with a boy or girl

Chasing your dreams is what youth is for
Try opening and closing many doors
Let your dreams lead you to places untold and
See your excitement and yearning for more unfold

Don't waste time, time waits for no one
Follow those dreams so you'll have no regrets
Dreams can come true and you'll have a
Life time of memories you'll never forget

Control

With her sultry eyes, she gave me that look
Her body spoke volumes in that black cat suit
She has to leave with me tonight
I will accept nothing less

I took her home, so we could be alone
She turned me on and she took control
Straddling my thighs, she placed
Soft kisses upon my eyes

In all her naked glory, she took control
I felt my manhood unfold
I lost my mind as I stroked her smooth behind
She took me to heights I have never known

Caught up in her swollen lips
I enjoyed myself all night long
The next morning, on my way home
I made up excuses to tell my wife

Of course she'll be mad I was out all night
She has lots of diamonds, furs or brand new cars
From all the other nights I had to make it right

I'll go broke keeping a happy wife
So I can have a happy life!

Cynthia Young

Come Together

Vows are made under a clear blue sky and
He looks at her with a gleam in his eyes
They are in love and it's easy to see
They have come together as man and wife

Young and in love they faced the trials and tribulations
That came their way. Working hard and playing hard
They built a life together day by day

Mid-life crisis strikes and he loses his mind
Leaving his faithful wife behind
She is not fazed; she knows his fling won't last
She doesn't wait for him, and does her thing

Time goes by and they rekindle their love
Past mistakes are forgiven; because life is short
They make up for lost time and never look back
They come together and make a new pack

Dead Beats

Dead Beats are not just Dad's, there are Mom's too
Children are going without; waiting on a check
For the things they need like food, clothing and presents
Under the Christmas tree

Society steps in to help the children out
Providing for their necessities
While the Dead Beats are no where around
Lost to the images of their children growing
By leaps and bounds

Dead Beats step up and take care of your responsibilities
Don't pawn your children off on society

Sometimes these Dead Beats come back into their
Children's lives, making promises they never keep
The children know; they've heard them before
So they hide their faces in their hands and weep

Dead Beats step to the plate, it doesn't have to be too late
Make a difference in your child's life
They need your love and support and providing
Diapers and day care just isn't enough

Kisses, hugs, tickles and giggles and being tucked into bed
Give your little ones happy thoughts and images of you
That will forever remain in their heads

Cynthia Young

Disrespect

It's not often nowadays that you hear a young person
Say, yes ma'm or no sir, dude is the word of the day
Along with that, a lot of young people don't go out of their way

They don't offer a hand or open a door
That's not what this generation does anymore, there's
No modesty in the clothes they wear as they head out the door
You'll hear young men cussing and calling a woman a whore

Disrespectful, talking to their parents like they're friends
Young girls winking and blinking at older men
Young men hanging around gas stations and liquor stores
Don't give a damn about a job, all they know is how to keep
An eye out for the next mark to rob

No respect for what others own, not eager
to learn, no education puts them
At a disadvantage to earn, leaving them
hopeless to compete in this world
But they damn sure know all of a rap songs harsh words

Education earned in the streets, keeps them alert and on their feet
No diploma from school, doesn't make them fools
They easily know the value of snow, how to count
Their money and the difference between a gram and a kilo

Don't Wonder

I don't want you to wonder
I want you to know from the deepest
Depths of my being, that I love you so

Never wonder about how much I care
You can take my love
Devotion and loyalty everywhere
Anywhere day or night
Even when life takes its final flight

Don't wonder, I want you to know
I will always stand with you
Because I love you so

Cynthia Young

Don't Be In a Hurry

Don't be in a hurry to rush through life, stop and
Consider your next move twice

When we are young we can't wait to get older
So we rush to do things that make us feel bolder

We should remember that we are where we should be
At the moment we are there, fate has a way of keeping
Us in check, but we always think we know best

Hurrying through the traffic, cursing because it's slow
Never thinking that there is a reason for it you don't know

A blessing in disguise could be right before your eyes
But you might not recognize it if you're moving too fast

Slow down and listen, you may need to hear what someone
Has to say and learn something new that will help
You get through the day

You didn't catch the airplane; you missed it by a minute
Just think how lucky you are not to be in it
Sitting next to an obnoxious man, fighting off his
Wandering hands

Don't be in a hurry to rush out of the house, without
Leaving your loved one with a tender touch
Loving words and a juicy kiss on the mouth

Life is rushing by us as it is, slow your roll
And live for the moment you're in
Take a deep breath, listen to your inner voice and
You'll always make the proper choice

Draw the Line!

He calls late at night on his 15 minute break
He wants to come by for a booty call
He says "Please baby stay awake"

He comes and goes and calls when he can, he
Feels like he can do what he wants; because he's the man

However, a pattern starts to emerge just when it's
Time for those special occasions to occur

Suddenly, nothing is right. There are no calls on his
Break late at night. He hasn't called in weeks
His phone is going to voicemail, what the hell!
He is totally out of reach

He calls when the special occasion is over with
A mouth full of excuses and an argument begins
He's making it seem like you are the blame and
He never stops trying to run his game

He talks plenty of smack, "Baby, I want to
Come over" still no reason why he didn't
Call or come before and that is your cue
To tell his ass you don't need him anymore

Keep it moving don't let him steal your joy
Disappointing you time after time, while you wait
And wish he would call and come through the door

He's been taking you for granted for a very long time
Stop the madness girl and draw the line!

Cynthia Young

Embrace Me

I want to be embraced by you, loved, caressed
And hugged by you

These things mean more to me than gifts of gold
These things will never get old

I want you to embrace not just my body but
My mind as well, I respond with laughter and
Joy whenever you touch me, can't you see
These are the most important things to me

Hold me and kiss me, I long for you to embrace me

Enough!

He doesn't hear when I talk to him, he walks away
From me on his way to the gym

He's crazy and wild since he left me and his child
His calls are scary and I am wary that he will
Hurt me one day, he says he has nothing
To lose, when he gets out of jail he's
Going to give me the blues

"Listen to me. Open your deaf ears losing
Job after job you never cared, you had
Your chance to make our house a home
Please! Just go away and leave me alone"

I called the cops and gave them the news
Guess what; there's nothing they can do until
He's beaten me to a pulp or has taken my life

Watching every corner, jumping at the phone
I have to protect me and my baby, we are all alone

I have had enough!
I refuse to be a victim, I will be the victor
He found that out the next time he busted through
My door. I lost my hook up and forgot I was his
Wife and I did not hesitate to take his sorry ass life!

Faking It

We met in the elevator and I caught him
Giving me the side eye. I spoke up and we
Made a date, I told him not to be late

After a great dinner and drinks we decided
To dash, bodies were heating up and
We went to his place to crash

His athletic build turned me on
Broad shoulders, tiny waist
Hugh thighs ripped and tight
I was looking forward to an
Exciting night

He did all the right things, he liked
Playing with my nipple ring
Neither one of us was shy and I
Thought, I picked the right guy

I was in for a shock when he
Pulled off his pants, his tool was
The size of my thumb and
Could barely be seen; this was
Turning out to be a bad dream

He didn't realize the rest of his manhood
Was sucked up inside that athletic build

He tried and tried; but he could not make me squeal
So I laid there and faked it so good, there was no
Way he'd know, his little man really wasn't a big deal

Flipping

No one does anything good enough for you
You never acknowledge the things I do but
You'll praise strangers who barely know you

You flip out on people close to you without
Provocation, never truly explaining what is wrong
You just continue to sing your sad song

Everything is always about you. Never
Admitting to the things you do, a dark cloud
Constantly follows you. You flip from foul to nice
At the drop of a hat, what's up with that?

You flip out about this or that, everyone
In your eyes is to blame and you are
Always calling people out of their names

Everyone's not stupid just so you know
Other people are doing just fine
You're the one out of step with the flow

When will you learn all that flipping out is
Not really what life is about. Humble yourself
Get your priorities straight and please find it
In your heart to let go of your deep seated hate
And maybe your life will turn around
Before it's too late

Flutter

As he enters the club he catches your eye
He strides across the room in expensive shoes
He is very fly and he makes you flutter
As he passes you by

Your eye lashes flutter, your belly flutters
And oh my, your insides do a dance
All the women surround him, is it possible
You could have a chance

Through the crowd he stares at you and
Nothing stops your knees from going weak
Here he comes; it's really you that he seeks

As he starts to speak, your words escape in a stutter
Everything about you is in a flutter

Tall, ripped and handsome as can be
He says he wants to dance with you
He pulls you close, very close and
You notice his body is fluttering too

Who knew, someone like him
Is feeling the same way you do

For Your Pleasure

I want to please you and do what you want me to do
Baby tell me how you want it and I will give it to you

Face down in the pillow, face to face, I want you to have
It in the right place, just the way you want it
Come on let's give it a go, I'm ready
To give you a nasty show

On the bed, on the table, in the corner
I have never been so damn horny. I'm here to please you
I'll do it all, c'mon let's do it up against the wall

Tell me what you want me to do, I have
Some new tricks for you, always willing to try
You are my girl and I am your guy

I love caressing your body tenderly
I love entering you gingerly and taking you
To the place you love to be and those sweet
Sounds you're making are all because of me

I'll give you what you want, where and when
You want it, any time you want it

It pleasures me to pleasure you, I'll always give you
My very best, I will make you happy or I will not rest

I'll take your climax off the chart and
When I feel you release and explode
Then and only then, will I release my load

Frenemy

Frenemy – a hybrid of friend and enemy

Are we genuinely friends or do you really deep down
Dislike me and you're just pretending to be my friend?

There always seems to be a rivalry that never ceases
There is a hint of hidden jealousy now and then
Doesn't that seem odd coming from a friend?

You cut me to pieces over the simplest things I do or say
Then you suddenly cover your tracks from this recent attack
Smile at me and pat me on the back

We are drawn to each other and we have our
Moments of accord, the next thing I know we're
Snapping out harsh words

It always seems like you're waiting and hoping I'll slip up
And that will make an opportunity for you to slide in some shade
Oh, make no mistake I get my digs in too, but I'm
Tired of playing these games with you

Watching my own back is really what I need to do
Because I'm never sure of what you might really be up to
I'll feed you from a long handled spoon
And believe me it's not a moment too soon

Friend

A Mother calls her friend to open up and vent
Her worry is something she can't hide, her
Friend listens intently to every word that is said

A Mother can't show her feelings; it's her job to stay strong
But when the house is empty she let's the tears flow
They stop abruptly, when she hears her child
Come through the door

It's hard for a Mother to see her only baby decline
Into an illness that boggles the mind
The friend listens intently; it breaks her heart too, to hear
How her friend is hurting; because she is very dear

Encouragement is what she offers through her own
Palpable fears, now is the time to be at the ready
To hold her friends hand, so she can stay steady

Ghetto Candy

Her name is Candy and she lives in the hood
She's a product of what other people say is no good
Dad left a long time ago; Momma pays the rent being a Ho
Baby brother went to jail again for cutting his woman on the chin

Life is different here in the hood; but Candy lives like a queen
Strutting around in her skin tight jeans, ribbons of gold-red
Extensions showing in her hair, false nails in bright colors
That blinds the eye. She steps to the car with a bag of grass
She vowed to herself she would not be the one selling her ass

She's seen how people live on the other side of town
She's in this ghetto life right now and it is what it is
But she refuses to let it get her down. Surviving day in
And day out, one day at a time, when you live in
The ghetto that's all you ever have on your mind

She sells her stash and has plenty of cash to move to another level
She's going to beat the devil and move far away. She plans
To come back and pull someone else from this ghetto prison
So they too can experience a different kind of living

Like millions of other young teens Ghetto Candy is in the
Prime of her life with plenty of dreams, but she was cut down
In a hail of gunfire on her way to the other side of town
Now it's over for her as they lower her casket into the ground

Bullets flying, young people dying for no reason at all
Black and Brown and that's not all who want to see the
Violence end, so there will be no more Ghetto Candy's
Losing out on their dreams

He Didn't Tell Me

I just found out he didn't tell me
He's been married every since he's been with me
I thought he was my man exclusively

But it turns out that he cheated on me with his wife
I defended him to my girls, they never thought
He should even be in my world

Now all I want is for him to be out of my life
I gladly want him to go back to his wife

He didn't tell me, he secretly taped us
Having sex while he and his wife
Sat back and counted the zeroes on the check

I feel hurt and disgusted as I walk away
He is the lowest of the low, that's
What I found out today

Yes I got laid, I got played, but in the end, I got paid!

Cynthia Young

His Smiling Eyes

From the moment I saw him standing in my front yard
With a body that was rock hard I was lost in his smiling eyes

At fifteen years old I suddenly realized I'd found a love
That would transcend time and he would
Always be somewhere in my mind

I could see myself drowning in his eyes, I melted
With just a look from him, that's all it took
I never wanted to leave his side, fate
Took us in different directions and
We no longer expressed our affections

I've always had a special place for my one and
Only high school crush, for I will always have fond
Memories of meeting him the very first day

I will summon him to my mind and I will lose
Myself in his smiling eyes as I remember the love
I had for him until the day he died

Honey I'm Home

I was naked at the door when he came home from work
I kissed him and began to unbutton his shirt
He started to protest; but I covered his mouth and throat
With kisses, he dropped his head back, closed his eyes
And moaned softly, as I stroked between his thighs

I don't want tame sex; I want a rough ride tonight
He put his hand on my ass and I whispered grab it
Grab my ass and hold it tight, spread it, rub it
Grind it and let me know you love it

Grab it and find my groove, move inside me
With your talented tool, back and forth
To and fro, rub it, grind it, hold it; pump it
Ride it, smack it and let your white lava flow
Bite my lip and whisper you love me
Then come back for more

Now, what was it you wanted to say when you
Walked through the door?

Cynthia Young

I Need a Job

No sooner than I bought my house I got papers that
Said I was laid off, not one to dwell on bad
News I got off my butt and put on my shoes

Looking for a job is a job and it ain't easy
Beating the streets and sending out resumes
Takes up all of my day

One road block after the other from the
Unemployment office, to applying online
This job search takes up all of my time

I don't want to stand in the unemployment line
I want to punch a clock and work eight hours
To get mine

I need a job so I can spend time working
In my garden, not being on hold on
The telephone line

I'll make an effort every day, knowing that
Eventually something will come my way
I won't look back at what use to be

I know something out there is better than
What I had and keeping that in mind
I can't get mad

One door closed, another one will open
Taking me to new heights, new beginnings
And no more sleepless nights

Insatiable Thirst

He sat in a big comfortable leather chair as the breeze
Blew the curtains and ruffled his hair

Smoke curled around his head as he focused his
Attention on the big round bed

With silk scarves binding her wrists
A beautiful woman lay there spread eagle
While another one's head bobbed between her legs

Their writhing and moans and their smooth skin
Dripping with sweat soon made the man
Want to join in

He felt heat creeping up his thigh and
His manhood began to rise

Women fascinated him and were sexy indeed
But there was another choice he did not overlook
One of these beauties was in disguise and had an
Undeniable hook

Tonight, he would have the one with the warm pink center
Just waiting for him to enter *and* the one that looked like him

His only dilemma was which one he would mount first
And which way; from the back or the front
It really didn't matter he was just anxious to quench his
Insatiable sexual thirst

Cynthia Young

Irreplaceable Love

(In memory of my parents)

My mother and father were my very first loves
My first protectors, teachers and cheerleaders
That came from heaven above
So they could show me unconditional love

All through my life, they stood with me
Guiding and encouraging what I should do
Shaping my mind, to be strong and self sufficient
They prepared me for life's challenges without conditions

Even with the mistakes I've made, they picked me up
And came to my aid, leaving me with their
Wisdom to move forward and learn from my
Experiences every day

When they are gone, grief runs deep, the tears and woeful
Groans of my sorrow erupt from within, as I come to realize
No one will ever love me the way they did and
Give me that irreplaceable love that they never hid

It's Been a Long Time

It's been a long time since I've seen you my friend
Even though we have not spoken you always
Crossed my mind

Life has taken turns left and right and eventually
Made us lose sight. But social media has done
A good thing, it has found you and we
Are back together again

Laughing and reminiscing about our past and
Looking forward to more time together
Into the future with no time to spare
As each one of gets older and
Fights back the grey hair

It's been a long time and we will search for
Others we miss; meanwhile we will
Keep these renewed friendships
Alive and enjoy each others company
For the rest of our lives

Cynthia Young

Just Cry

When I saw you today I could see the hurt in your eyes
I saw them swimming with tears

Just cry, I said and let it out
You were married for many years
You don't have to stop the tears
Just cry and let it out

You'll have feelings of separation that
You feel can't be mended
You'll have many days like this
Until time begins to heal the rift

Be thankful for the years he was yours
When he stood by your side and helped
With little things like the daily chores

Relish in the memories of how he looked at
You so lovingly and smiled when
You entered the room

He's in your heart and he'll always be there
Even though he's not in his favorite chair

Don't hold back, let it out
It will take time to heal, meanwhile
Your tears will continue to ebb and flow

Your chest will swell and fall heavy and hard
Breathing will be labored, your thoughts will swirl
As you hear yourself moan, how will I go on?

Just cry, and let it out, eventually your heart
Will mend and believe it or not you will heal
So, cry and let it out 'til then

Karma

Karma is a bitch, is what people say
When people do you wrong, trust and believe
They will have their day

You may not be around to see it happen, but
Karma keeps track and knows when to strike
It never forgets, even though they might

When someone is mean and nasty, hateful and rude
Always walking around with an attitude
Spewing foul words at you out of their mouth

Just know they can't be happy and they'll
Have plenty to say, just step to the side and
Get out of their way

Karma is a bitch, oh yes, it is and anyone who
Thinks they can avoid it really hasn't lived

However you choose to live your life
Good or bad, Karma knows what to do
Sorrow or joy is what's in store for you

So think about your actions and keep
Karma in mind, because you better believe
You'll reap what you sow over time

Cynthia Young

Leave Nothing Unsaid

She lay there dying in her bed, her children
Standing around her thinking to themselves
What else needs to be said?

Thinking back over the years, how their mother
Wiped their tears; all the spats they had
Never amounted to much, what they
Remembered now, was her gentle touch

Mother's love was what they craved as they
Walked beside the casket to the grave
Never again would they hold her close
Her gentle touch is what they would miss the most

They cherished her while she lived, giving
Her anything and everything they could give
Their inconsolable grief ran rampant in
Their hearts and heads

The children were satisfied that they had
Left nothing unsaid

They've never known this kind of grief, but knowing
She no longer suffered brought them some relief

Now she will get peace and comfort from the Lord
They realized she did what she came here to do
And the children were left on one accord

Lesson on Love

Rainy days are made for love; it makes me want to cuddle
Soft music fills the room. Grey skies make you slow your roll
This pleasure could last for hours untold

Rainy days make me feel like making love on
A soft fluffy bear skin rug. I poured honey all over
His body, I'm going to lick him all over and
I won't leave a trace; I love the way he tastes

We get naked and I guide his head and
Hands and encourage his strokes, he's
Getting good at this; he no longer chokes

The rain beats hard against the window pane
He finds his rhythm and hits my spot and
Through my sounds of joy I call his name
After today, I won't call him my boy toy

He has learned to love me like a real man
The three minute man is no more; because I
Taught him my secret to doing the deed
He discovered you don't need excessive speed

Cynthia Young

Love

What is Love?
Love is an overused word. Don't tell me that you
Love me and not show me! Love requires action
And actions speak louder than words

What good is it when you say you love me?
But you beat me and throw me down
What good is it when you say you love me?
But you disrespect me all over town

Your words hurt and cut like a knife
A love like yours makes me think of
Running away or taking my life
Because I can not endure another day
Of your hateful, deceitful ways

Love should not hurt it should uplift, empower
And support, bringing laughter and joy
Not fear and disgust

Just saying I love you to hear yourself talk
Makes me know you are not willing to
Walk the walk

Love requires positive actions that make
Me know, that you truly mean what you say
Loving words and actions must coincide and
Come from a spiritual place deep down inside

Loyalty

Loyalty, a seven letter word cuts
To the core whenever it is heard

Loyalty, transcends the likes of
Royalty and extends to husbands, wives
Friends and family

Loyalty, is what I have for those that
Are important to me

It is one of the deepest threads
That runs through your life, it is more
Valuable than money or fame

Loyalty, is what upholds the
Essence of your spirit and your name

Men

Beautiful men all around me, men I love
To watch, especially when I know they are watching me

Big men, short men and tall men like
Al, John, Butch and George, high school sweethearts
That ruled the courts

Men in suits and men in shorts
Make a woman take notice when he enters a room
He starts to rap and she wants to make him her groom

Men in fast cars, men standing in bars scoping out the room
Men, on the bus or in the Motown studio singing a tune

Hard working men, smart men even the nerdy guy
Begins to look good as a boyfriend

But, the bad boys always seem to catch our eye and
They are the ones we go for first, never mind
The fact he's taking money from your purse and
Using your car until it grinds to a halt with thirst

We look for the good guys, but they're not wearing white hats
It's easy to pass them by especially when that bad boy
Just blacked your eye

Men, we can't live without them or so we think; let me
Think about that while I have another drink

Midnight Sky

I looked up at the midnight blue sky with a twinkle in my eye
Stars sparkled and glowed bright in the darkness of night

A warm breeze rippled through the tall swaying palm trees and
Whispered softly to soothe me, my body relaxed, my mind cleared
And released the pent up stress of many years

The beauty of the night was all around me, the sweet fragrance
Of Jasmine heightened my sense of smell and I
Heard the soft wistful sounds of the Nightingale

Water trickled and pooled in the pond while the darkness
Engulfed the outline of Big Bear Mountain

I stared at the stars hoping to see Mars and the Constellation
Was bold and bright on that very quiet peaceful night

The Centaur stood ready with his bow to shoot an arrow
I imaged he wouldn't miss and anything he shoots
Will be touched with bliss

As my eyes grew heavy with sleepiness
I took one last look

The quarter moon was the main attraction in the beautiful sky
Shaped like a thumbnail with a French white manicure
I could tell, that's how God liked to do her nails

Cynthia Young

Momma Said

In memory of my mother
(September 1927 – August 2012)

When I was a little girl, my momma helped shape my world
Even now, sometimes I can hear her words

Momma said, "Baby never leave the house with dirty
Underwear, in case you get in an accident"
So, she always sent me out with clean clothes
And bows and ribbons in my hair

Momma said, "Have your butt on the front porch
Before the streets lights come on" and that is
Exactly what I do today, even though I am grown

Momma said, "I brought you in this world
And I will take you out!" Because I sassed
Her and that made her mad

Momma said, "Go get me a switch off the tree"
Ahh, man! I knew she was going to tear into me

Momma said, "I heard that!" when I mumbled under
My breath because she told me to go to bed, Jesus!
I thought; that woman has ears in the back of her head

When all was said and done after my prayers, she hugged and
Kissed me and said "Good night Baby I love you"
As she tucked me into bed

These are just a few of many that I know from an era
When your parents would take you to task and
Didn't think twice about knocking you on your ass

Morning Love

The morning dew still clung to the grass as the sunlight
Made it sparkle like beautiful chunks of broken glass

The coffee brewed and the aroma filled every room in the house
There were soft sounds of love from a couple still in bed
Playing with the covers over their head

He woke her with a nice surprise, excitement and longing
Gleamed in her eyes

His manhood was hard and curved, she took control
Swirling her kisses in rhythmic motions, he rubbed
Her like his magic lamp and could feel
Her getting damp

Love abound they found their common spot and
Together their friction exploded with her on top
Drained she fell forward on his chest, he never
Disappointed her, mornings were the best

They lingered in the moment and held each other tight
Kissing and planning to take their morning love into the night

Cynthia Young

Mr. Dirt

We see him on the street with tattered torn clothing
With dirt on his shirt and rags wrapped around his feet

His hair is matted and his beard has had no care
We see these Mr. Dirt's everywhere; on the street corners
Holding a cardboard sign, shuffling their way to your car for a dime

A shopping cart carries what he holds dear
That is why he keeps it near
We walk past and lean away, hoping nothing touches us as
We go about our busy day

He begs you for a cigarette and your extra change to help him out
He stands on the corner hustling our dimes then leaves the corner
For better times

Mr. Dirt has quite the hustle and counts the money
Collected from his crew; on his way to his hidden ride
A big white S Class Mercedes is what he drives
He paid for it with the money he got from you

Now that you see what a scam street corner hustling can be
Hold on to your dimes and don't feel sorry for Mr. Dirt

He's probably living better than you are in a house on
A hill and you better believe, there is no dirt
On his tailor made silk shirts

No Teenage Playbook

Teenage years can be exciting, experimental and very confusing
Trying to look cool to your friends, sometimes causes
You to use drugs and sex to see what it's like

Teenage pregnancy is on the rise, babies
Trying to raise babies don't
Have a clue, there's no playbook to tell them what to do

Listening to friends and not to your parents
Following in the footsteps
Of a favorite celebrity, you dress in clothes that make you look old

Parents don't always know what to do an
Open line of communication
Is what they want from you. Teenagers think parents are too old
To know what teenagers go through; never thinking they use
To be teenagers once too

There is no teenage playbook to tell you society can be cruel
Getting bullied in school, suicide, self mutilation and
Putting your finger down your throat makes
You hide your sick body under a big raincoat

Don't be pressured to have sex, disease is still around and
There are plenty of teenagers at free clinics all over town

Go to school and learn the alphabet don't try to be grown to soon
You can make mistakes that will cause you serious regrets

If there was a playbook, you might save yourself some grief
Meanwhile, listening to your parents is the best thing
To help you get relief

Cynthia Young

Old School Lovers

An old school lover makes love to every part of your body
With smooth experienced moves that have been perfected over time

They don't just make love to your body. They make love to your mind
Whispering longing, lingering sweet words
That tell you how much you mean and how much you're worth
Over a glass of red wine

They like to flirt and play, nothing is better than loving this way
Listening to your wildest dreams, surprising you with a lavish
Dinner at the end of your day

He rubs your feet, strokes your hair and
Places soft kisses everywhere
Sharing, caring, making love throughout the night
Words need not be spoken as you hold each other tight
When you feel the beat of each others hearts
You know then, you never want to be apart

He's loved you for decades whether you thought you were looking
Cute or not, with your grey hair, hot flashes, wrinkles and age spots
Old school lovers see past all those things and embraces
And cherishes the woman he gave his ring

One Night Stand

They met on a street car, their chemistry is smoking
It can't be denied. Public displays of affection
Are the images they left in everyone's eyes

The heat between them reaches blast
He knows he has to tap that ass
She's hot and steamy, she's never been
With anyone this dreamy

They smash and smash all night long
Doing the damn thing to her favorite song
On top, on the bottom, side ways
Against the wall, they didn't miss a beat
They did it all

The break of dawn, chases away the night
Homeboy is dressed and ready to take flight
She wants him to stay and continue to play

Cynthia Young

He hit it and now it's time to quit it. He's
Not the spooning type, their one night
Stand was over last night

She's left behind, with his touch on her mind
But one thing is for sure, she got what she
Wanted too, before he left out the door

She wasn't looking for a man to stay, she learned
Long ago, not to let her feelings get in the way
There won't be any tears or stalking phone calls
And text messages throughout the day

She acted like a woman and played tricks like a man
Just goes to show you two can play that game!

He thinks he got over he thinks he's the man!
She has the last laugh though, because he
Really was the one night stand

Peep Show

I see you standing in your window and
You are staring back at me. I am startled by your
Nakedness and watch as you begin to play

I think to myself, this is exactly the way I like starting my day
You begin with slow moves to some unheard groove as
You toss your hair into the air

You caress your breast and I can only imagine how silky
Your skin is and I want to touch you very much

You turn your back and touch your toes; this is a move
I can tell that you know very well

From the back, I am mesmerized at the space between your thighs
I am numb, yet my body begins to respond to the sight and
I stand in the window well into the night

You fascinated me with all of your moves, especially the one —
Well you know, the one that hit me hard and I was done

Now, every time I pass my window I look your way, hoping to have
Another wonderful day; but this time with your invitation to
Come over and play

Cynthia Young

Pink Survivors

Inspired by Barbara Jo Young
Dedicated to Survivors Everywhere

Pink Survivors have lost their hair, sit for hours in a
Comfortable chair, to fight a battle we can't even imagine

She has endured unspeakable pain; but still her positive
Attitude and smile remain

Through her pain, she bravely encourages
And consoles you
You would not expect that, with all she's been through

Pink Survivor hats off to you, it takes a strong
Confident woman to do what you do

A Pink Survivor comes out on the other side
Looking forward to another chance at life

Resuming her role as mother, sister, friend and wife
Using her experiences to look forward and not back

She is no longer tattered and worn, sad
Or blue, her head is held high
She reaches out to others to help them along
Providing a strong shoulder for them to lean on

Pretty Eyes

The Pretty Eyes are all glammed up
Beautiful colors and jewels adorn what they see
They are wise and knowing and
Their first look of the day always, delves inside of me

Pretty Eyes in a beautiful face, what secrets do you disguise
Sadness, laughter, happiness and joy
The Pretty Eyes have seen these things before

Pretty Eyes smile through the years, along the journey of life
Shedding lots of tears, once wide eyed an innocent, saw
Innocence fade away

Pretty Eyes speak volumes without saying a word and can
Cut through a man without raising a hand

Years bring more knowledge that is kept inside, but
You can see that wisdom shine through the Pretty Eyes

Cynthia Young

Punishment

I've paid my dues but you continue to give me the blues
I'm not perfect I make mistakes, but no matter
How I atone, you continuously punish me
Every day I wake

Passive aggressive is what you are; undercover with your actions
Smooth with your shade and cutting remarks, it seems
I'll never get this target off my back —
Your punishment is slow and very exact

I've learned some lessons in life that will forever stay in my head
And I will endure your punishment, but make no mistake
I will not continue to beg

Rainbow Love

A woman loves another woman, a man loves another man
It shocks people sometimes to see them embrace and hold hands

Love knows no gender, color or race, it transcends
Barriers and injustices that these lovers often face

Enduring atrocities that come from hate, they
Have become stronger as each battle is won
Fighting for their cause has made them very strong

A force to be reckoned with, their pride is
Known around the world, as a boy loves a boy
And a girl loves a girl

They may be different but yet they want the same
Equality, health insurance and the same last name

Love binds them together, just like a straight couple
They want recognition that their love is real
Their love is true, even though they may not
Be the same as you

Cynthia Young

Retro Christmas in Detroit

Awakening to crystal white snow twinkling
In the daylight, pristine and untouched by footsteps
Gave me special delight

Today, I will see the Thanksgiving Parade
Bundled tight, Mom and I headed out to get a good spot
On the Woodward Avenue parade route

After the parade we stood in line to see
Hudson's Department store's magical, mystical
Santa's Workshop that amazed and excitement me

The animated dolls in the window displays
Made me want to stand there all day

We rushed to the 12th floor to see the Winter Wonderland
Toys galore were all around the floor, bright colored
Candy canes and so much more, Christmas Carol
Held my hand so I wouldn't lose my way
After all, it was my turn to sit on Santa's lap today

On the way home we could smell the freshly made caramel corn
As it began to snow, Mom and I rushed back home to replay
Our wonderful day, sitting around our Christmas tree and
Drinking hot chocolate, was a dream come true for me

Christmas day is here at last and I am overjoyed
Santa was good to me and brought me all my toys
My orange Tom Thumb typewriter in its own carrying case
Is the height of my joy and it goes with me every place

My mother helped to shape these wonderful memories
I still remember shopping for gifts at Crowley's, B. Siegel's and Sears
Mom continued this routine throughout my childhood years

Finally, we gathered at Aunt Helen's house for more presents and
Dinner with family and friends, this was the perfect way
For my favorite holiday to end

Cynthia Young

Revenge is Sweet

His phone is ringing, the screen lights up, I walk
Over and pick it up, right before my eyes
Is a picture he didn't bother to disguise of
An exotic woman with long dark hair and a
Sensual smile and a hot longing stare

I answer the phone and say "Hello." "Who are you?"
She wants to know. "I'm his girlfriend
We live together, my name is Heather"

She starts to curse and call me names, I shout
Back and also defame, when we calm down
There is a whole lot we want to know
"Don't be mad at me, be mad at him, he's the one
That lead you on, I'm the one he's cheating on"

We get together and have lunch to decide what to do about him
He's not going to get away with this scheme
We're out for revenge

We confront him in the shower, so he can't run away. When he
Sees us together he's not even fazed. He invites us in to get wet
He's thinking, threesome and hot nasty sex

We took off our spiked heels and whacked that ass
This is one shower he'll never forget. When we
Were done he certainly knew I was not the one
I pulled out my phone, took a picture and sent a Tweet
Our revenge was sweet and complete

He's out in the streets looking for the next girl to meet
Ladies, when you meet this handsome guy and
He shows you his physique, remember my Tweet

You'll recognize the big jagged "C" carved in his chest
And with that, I think you can figure out the rest

Runaway

Young, restless, hard headed and alone you are
On your way to Hollywood; a long way from home

Fear starts to set in when you are approached by
Scary looking men, no money and no food
It was easy to fall prey to whatever these
Men had to say

Standing on the street corner you attract the eye
Of the highest bidder with the most money
To buy

Too much make-up, skirts too high, drugs take the
Edge off and rose colored glasses are how you see
This life is not where you want to be

Swirling thoughts of a broken home, missing the friends
That never made you feel alone. Teachers that pressed
You to achieve, you can't understand why you
Didn't want that, now you wish you were back

Rescued and happy to be home, the experiences
You've had are second to none, it has made you
Really appreciate your hard working Mom

Never again will you think about running away
Your experiences make you more
Appreciative of what you have today

Your future looks bright. Just remember, the
Experiences from your past, help shape you into
The person that you are and will become. So don't
Feel guilty about any of it, it's over and done

Scary Movies

Dedicated to my extended family
Virgie, Charles, Kenny, Joyce, Jerry and Chubby

I looked forward to summertime and I couldn't wait to
Come to your house and spend the summer with you
We had slumber parties with covers on the floor
We were excited to our core

Every Friday night we gathered in the
Living room around the TV with Jiffy Pop Popcorn
To watch Boris Karloff and Vincent Price

We watched through our fingers as the
Mummy slowly dragged his leg
And caught up with another man. Swamp
Thing, Werewolf, Dracula and
The Creature from the Black Lagoon, was enough to keep us up
All night huddled together in one room

The long dark hallway to the bathroom held shadows we could see
And made us think that we'd rather hold our pee

Cynthia Young

When we went to the basement to get clothes
Off the line, fear ran through our bodies; we still had fresh
Images of Frankenstein etched in our mines

We linked our arms and slowly descended, scared and
Breathless our hearts beating out of our chests
We looked for monsters to jump us from under the stairs

Those were the days of red and grape Kool-Aid, syrup sandwiches
Jump rope, metal roller skates and hopping
On one foot on the front porch
We laughed and played all summer long, then suddenly is was time
For me to go back home

When I watch a scary movie now, I will think of you. The
Wonderful summers we had having fun and our silliness
Because these are the things about you, I truly miss

Second Chances

As we live our lives day by day it's not hard for us to lose our way
Mistakes made are sometimes the opportunity we need to
Learn something we didn't know; something that will
Help us to grow

Some of us are fortunate to get a second chance and re do
Our flow

Second chances should never be taken for granted, seize the
Moment and take advantage of the chance you've been given
It could change the life you're living

People don't often give second chances to another that has
Messed up. Those mistakes can turn out to be tough
Losing a love, friendship or relationship with family
Will take extra effort and special remedies

Prayer, truth, respect, honesty and sincerity may be
Needed depending on the circumstance. Even then
That might not be enough to get you a second chance

Cynthia Young

Sex Addiction

She never blends in, she always stands out
Luscious full lips that she loves to pout
Beautiful almond shaped eyes, smoldering
Like red hot embers from deep down inside
She's on the prowl and there is no shame in her game
When it comes to her addiction, she has no pride

She exudes sex appeal that is relentless
Sensual feelings bubble up from her core
She thinks of sex all the time; nothing more
The vision of his body on hers takes control

She is addicted to her desire for sex, her body craves the
Constant rush and that is how the addiction came to be
She wants a well endowed man to quench her needs
She has to have the warmth of his mouth and seed

Addicted to sex, not love, she searches
For sex and not love; because love hurts
And sex never does, it's the pleasure
She craves, not someone to love

Licking, rubbing, groaning, penetrating
Arching her back to meet his thrust, then releasing
With wild screams of joy, she sighs as she reaches
To touch the wetness between her thighs. Her body quivers
As she regains control, it's at times like this she loses her soul

Oh yes, this is what she lives for every day, all day
Sultry as hell, she uses what she has
To get the men she needs day after day
She has one question.....

Do you want to play?

Shopping Addict

You're shopping in the middle of the night
The shopping channels have your credit card
Limits looking a fright

It's so easy you can't resist, from jewelry
To pots and pans just press okay on the
TV remote and a few days' later boxes
Show up at your door

You know the delivery man by his first name
You can't look him in the eye because you
Are ashamed

Hiding packages all over the house you're hoping
You can keep them hidden from your spouse
Only you find out that he's shopping too
Now, he surely can't say anything to you

Why bother with the shopping malls
Traffic, crowds and long lines
When you can pick up your phone with your
Pajamas on and never have to leave home

You're addicted to this new way of shopping any time
Any day, all day, it's just what you don't need
Who cares, life is too short get what
You want that's why you go to work!

Side Chick

A side chick gets with your man any way she can
Even though she knows he's a married man
She thinks she is bad enough to pull him and
Put on the wedding band

Side chicks know what they have to endure
Never seeing him on holidays. Watching him leave
To take his kids out to play. He never stays over
She accepts his whispered call for phone sex
In the middle of the night. He never takes
Her out in public, she is just a secret lover

Never wanting to rock the boat, she keeps her
Disappointment hidden in her throat; asking
Questions is a no no; but she wants more
She has to know about his wife and
Follows him to see where he will go

Watching him share kisses with his wife
She flips and blows her lid and tells him what
She witnessed standing behind the tree, she yelled
At him "You're making a fool out of me!"

He snapped back, "You are a side chick
Nothing more. So stay in your lane, whore!
I just wanted to hit it, to satisfy my wick

"I had no intentions of leaving my wife
I'll be with her for the rest of my life
My wife knows I like to play every
Now and then; but she also knows I
Always come home to her in the end!"

Silence

The silence is all around me, no laughter, or talking
The way it used to be

I've never felt so alone in our home
Tears come and go and now silence is all I know

I listen intently to hear your voice
But you've gone on, you had no choice
The silence enrobes my thoughts. I miss you more
Than I can say, I think about how you loved me
Night and day

Eventually, I will leave our home even though
I feel your spirit all around and it makes me feel like
I want to stay; but life goes on and I need to find my way

As the silence begins to fade my dear
I want you to know, that I will
Take your spirit with me, wherever I go

Cynthia Young

Stuck in a Rut

In the beginning when things were exciting
And new, you couldn't keep your hands
Off each other, dancing and drinking
At home in the nude

Years go by and things slow down
Now it's a chore to even get your sexy on
Sleep by nine o'clock you have
No desire to make the bed rock
Looks like you're stuck in a rut

Kids, jobs, bills and the like
Take a heavy toll, as you sit up nights
Trying to figure out a way to make ends meet
There is no time to hang out in the streets
Looks like you're stuck in a rut

Boring and dull nothing exciting
Goes on in your life anymore
You can even go to sleep with an
Open bedroom door

Rooms apart, everyone in their own chair
Nobody cares about letting down their hair, forget
Getting your party on, those days are long gone

You're just too boring and stuck in a rut
To get off your butt and have any fun

Superficial Girl

A superficial girl, says she wants a real man
But all she does is hold out her hand for what she
Can get; to her every man looks like a trick

What's up with that – try something new
Stop looking at the exterior, how's
That been working for you

Try looking into a man's heart and soul
What kind of car he drives and the
Style of his clothes has gotten real old
She is so superficial

She wants a man who can pay her bills
Buy her fancy clothes, purses and shoes
She got those things and a whole lot of the blues

She wants a rich guy no matter how he looks
Fat, short or dumpy as long as his pockets
Are long, she'll be on the crook of his arm
She is so superficial

She wants a man for all the wrong reasons
And she'll only keep him for a short season
Superficial is the name of her game
She only wants the money, perks and fame

She says she wants a real man, but
A real man will see through her veil and
Avoid her like the plague to stay away from her hell

Surprise!

Surprise! Mom and Dad
I just dyed my hair pink, purple and red

Surprise! Mom and Dad
I'm pregnant by Tad, the jokes on me
'Cuz he doesn't want to be a Daddy

Surprise! Mom and Dad
I dropped out of school, so don't clean out my
Room, I'm on my way back home to live with you

Surprise! Mom and Dad
I'm not your baby boy anymore
I'm going out into the world; even
Though I know it won't be easy
As a pretty little girl

What's wrong Mom and Dad
Are these surprises too much for you to handle?

"No, child we're just fine, you'll have to have a
Better surprise than that to blow our minds"

"We raised you the best way we could
So, surprise! You'll have to own
Your choices and handle your business
And with that said we're all good!"

The Closet

I'm in the closet peeping out trying to see what gay life
Is all about, I'm still not sure if I want to come out

Mom and Dad won't be happy with me and
I know people will certainly judge me
Just because I want to be what deep down
Inside my soul tells me I should be

Should I come out, or not, should I come out, or not?
I really want to leave this closet life, I want to be
Myself in the broad daylight

The closet hides me and hears my confessions and it
Is where I keep my gay possessions

I want to come out, be out, shout out I'm gay and
I'm proud, I will, I'll come out – but maybe not
I don't know if I have the strength to deal

Time goes by and I realize, the closet imprisons me
I have grown and now I **know** that I will never be happy
If I don't live the life that is meant for me

I've left the closet and I am free! It no longer hides me
I am strong and confident, my head is held high
I'm out of the closet and I will be gay
Until the day I die!

Cynthia Young

The Dancer

She enters the stage, bright lights, music and a packed house tonight
Her costume sparkles and shows plenty of skin
It's what she has to wear to entice the men
She struts her stuff from side to side, gyrating and rolling
Her body up and down, round and round

Suddenly, she slithers to the pole and climbs real high and
Slides down slowly to catch every man and woman's eye
When she's done, money is laying all over the stage
She knows she is good at what she does and she is all the rage

Her nine to five doesn't pay as much, she has to work
The pole at night; so she can have money for lunch
School books are not cheap and bills must be paid
She makes sacrifices to have a better future one day

Life is good; she has left the pole behind
Her dancing days were hard but very kind
As she walks down the hall to her new office

CEO is what the sign says on her door
She sits in her big purple leather chair and
Reflects on what it was like to be poor

The pole served its purpose back in the day
It helped get her a better life. Now she's looking
Forward to becoming a Mother and maybe a Wife

The Oak Tree

He coaxed her to sit on his knee; he gave her cookies
And took her out behind the big oak tree

He'd been stroking her on the down low since she was eight
Doing things to her he didn't do to his mate
She became good at hiding her hate

One day soon, she would unleash it all
Her tears, fears, groans and moans would fall
From her throat like a wolf howling at the moon

All grown up the secret still lingers and flash backs
Of him and that oak tree, send her to the
Bottle for a long harsh bender

She returned to the place where the secret began
And pulled out her gun and confronted the man

She shot him in the head and left him dead
She wanted to make sure another child
Would not feel the way she did

She released the pain in her final hours
Soon she would be free and she would
Never again have to think about that oak tree

Cynthia Young

The Seventh Day

November 07, 2014
(My dad's Sunset)

My daddy was the first man I ever loved, I was his only child
I am so very grateful he was on this earth with me
For more than a little while

He laughed at his own jokes about other folks
And he loved telling stories about his life
To anyone that would listen; especially his wife

He returned to the land of his birth to nurture the
Lives of bovines, that grazed in the fields and
When he called her to feed; Miss Bo Bicky always
Came in from the hills

Tough as nails and smart as hell, he could speak
On subjects that were out of your reach
Daddy was always one that liked to teach

He loved guns and certainly had more than one
He could shoot the eye off a fly and he
Never missed at skeet, trophies piled up
Around his feet

Roaming the open roads in his RV he
Pretty much saw the things he wanted to see

On the seventh day, with a full moon in the sky
My dad closed his eyes, gave a sigh and
Left this world to really be free
Leaving behind Myrna, Tonia and me

The Wrong House

(Version I)

He watched her move from room to room
Day after day he came to know her every move

She lived alone and he watched patiently each day
As she left home, she never stayed gone very long

Weeks of watching went by; this would
Be easy she was a sitting duck
He decided to make his move. He tried
The window without much luck
It seemed to be stuck; then finally it gave way and
He eased inside into the darkness

He was just about to move around but before he could
He was hit upside his head with a baseball bat
She screamed at him, "I ain't no dummy suck'a
I've been watching you!"

When he woke up his hands and feet were cuffed to the bed
And he was in the buff; he had no idea his situation
Was about to get real rough

She was naked too and danced around in her birthday suit
She taunted him "Me and my crew are
Going to have our way with you"
He blacked out while they were doing the do

When she let him go, *he* called the cops and tried to explain the
Ass whooping he got from a buffed up lady that was in her 80's

His complaint had them laughing their asses off; because there was
No doubt, he'd met his match when he
tried to rob Miss Willie's house!

The Wrong House

(Version II)

He watched her move from room to room
Day after day he came to know her every move

She lived alone and he watched patiently each day
When she left home, she never stayed gone very long

Weeks of watching went by; this would
Be easy she was a sitting duck
He decided to make his move. He tried
The window without much luck
It seemed to be stuck; then finally it gave way and
He eased inside into the darkness

He was just about to move around but before he could
He was hit upside his head with a baseball bat
She screamed at him, "I ain't no dummy suck' a
I've been watching you!" She hit him again and told him
"I work out in the gym and I'm 82"

Cynthia Young

I plan to teach your ass a lesson, so next time you'll
Know what not to do!" and she proceeded to whoop that ass
Until he was black and blue

She taunted him all night long and finally it was the break of dawn
Did he make a big mistake and pick the wrong house?
Because this little grey haired lady had
stubble growing out of her face

When the police arrived she was standing by the door smoking
A thin cigar and sipping a glass of Whiskey
They high fived her and hauled him away
He found out he was no match for Ms. Willie on her worst day

Thick and Curvy

Thick is what I am, beautiful in my own skin
I am loved, hot and lusty by my man

Thick and curvy hips galore, my man
Is all over this body as soon as I
Walk through the door

I am in my element, sharp as a tack
My clothes hug every crevice and crack
Up and down my back

Skinny girls look out; I'm where it's at
Marilyn Monroe was curvy back in the day
Now, thick girls everywhere are becoming the rage

Runway skinny not too cool, but I ain't hating
Do what you got' a do
Just remember, men want booty they can grip
When they drive hard and deep

Feeling boney body parts can sure kill a hard
And make him rollover and go to sleep

Cynthia Young

Toys – Aren't Just For Kids

Toys are not just for kids, toys sometimes
Need to take the place of boys

They come in all shapes and sizes
Colors and textures too
You don't need a Harvard education
To know how they can please you

They vibrate you into another world
They can do what a boy can't do for a girl

Raincoats are optional
With or without it, the toy will still be
Functional leaving you with no worries

With your toy you never have to
Worry about being in a hurry

You can work a toy alone or not
Either way, they can make you hot
Wet and satisfied, leaving you breathless
Exhausted and thankful for the lone ride

Transition

I have come a long way from being a gang banger
In the streets of LA

Day after day, I rode through the hood
Pumping fists with my home boys
And doing no good

Jail time, showed me a life I didn't want to live
So I gave up my gang banging ways

I found love from a higher power
I give all praise now to the man
In the highest tower

I love the life I have now
Singing his praises through the hood
Teaching others how to do good

Cynthia Young

Twisted Heart

You smiled, laughed and talked real nice and had a
Pleasant face with one side light and the other side dark
Behind this face you spun your evil web of deceit and greed
To support your selfish needs

Veiled and dark, I discovered you had a twisted heart
Your thoughts and actions were more than enough to
Bring your twisted heart to light

You turned so quickly you were hard to recognize; but
As I look back I realized, you've always been in disguise
Believe me, now I have really opened my eyes

Trust and respect I have no more to give, without that
I must accept that you are foul and your soul has gone astray
We are no longer friends, I must step away

For you are not someone I choose to have in my life
Stepping back from you is the best thing for me to do

So I won't have to remove another knife from my back
Because of your dark and twisted heart and
The compassion and love I know you lack

Walk in My Shoes

Walk in my shoes before you judge and criticize
Because you really have not seen life through my eyes

You have not walked in my shoes, you have not lived my blues
So who are you to judge the things I've done?
Who said you should be the one to know
What is right and what is wrong

I've made mistakes, they come with living life
I won't be shamed because you don't approve
I won't look back and have regrets
Life's too short and on that you can place your bets

Live my life before you smugly think you know me
Maybe then and only then you can show me
That you would have made different choices; while listening
To the same voices, re living the same scenes
Stepping out of and not into your dreams

Don't judge and criticize me, until you have walked in my shoes
Lived my life and experienced my blues

Maybe I have not fulfilled your needs, maybe you want me
To be someone I can not be. It's easy for you to say
What should have been and what should be

I just want you to remember that you are
You and you can not be me

So try to see my truth through my eyes and embrace my blues
Maybe then you will have a glimpse of what it's like
If you ever have to walk my path in your own shoes

We Need to Talk

Sometimes men can be very hard to talk to and that
Can really frustrate the hell out of you
"We need to talk" strikes fear in a man's head
More than likely it's about a subject that he dreads

When can we get married, I want to have a baby
Why don't you spend more time with me
Why can't I go with you, I don't want to be alone
Why can't you just stay home?

What he hears is nagging and that drives men wild, they
Want to avoid these subjects and leave well enough alone
These are the conversations that make them
Want to run away from home

He'll tell you to relax and go with the flow
You're getting on his nerves and the next thing you know
He has an excuse to walk out the door

When he comes back, you've cooled off, once again
He managed to distract you from being in a huff

He knows you're not going to like his answers to your
Questions and he'll do anything to avoid the conversation

"We need to talk" puts pressure on his nerves, the last
Thing he wants is an argument with his girl

So when you see him become defensive make up
Your mind about what you really want; the answer to
Your questions or your man out on the hunt

Don't try to tie him down. Get some business of your own and
Watch him turn around. Believe me, then you won't have to worry
About being alone, he'll be happy to keep his ass at home

Wet

He gets me wet, even when I'm alone in my room
I close my eyes and I see him smiling as he
Sings my favorite tune

He gets me wet, when I think of him
Doing all the hot things he does to me
Sweat rolls off my body and puddles in the sheets
He is licking and kissing my feet, one toe
At a time, he blows my mind

He takes his time caressing my body all over
With his lips, then he slowly raises my hips
To touch, taste and feel what I have inside
Ohhh, it feels so good, I tightly close my eyes

Rubbing me down so gently, rubbing me like
I am his magic lamp. He really knows the
Secrets to keeping me damp

I am alone in my room, when he comes to me inside my head
He makes me wet and he's not even in my bed

Cynthia Young

What a Man Wants

I was sitting at the bar in the club when my attention
Was captured by a beautiful girl

Dressed in designer clothes, hair done with nice looking
Nails and toes, I decided this was a woman
I wanted to know

I offered her a drink and we enjoyed each others' company
She invited me to her home for the night
When I walked in what I saw gave me a fright

There were clothes, shoes and purses everywhere
Empty take out containers and lots of cat hair
This chick was nasty I just wanted to run

Her room and the bed was a mess
How in the hell could I even think about
Making love to her. I made excuses and
Told her I had to go

I was turned off and even as good as she looked
I was not about to land my hook; no way
Was I getting in bed with her; not knowing
If her hygiene was up to par, I got
In my car and went back to the bar

I needed a drink to think about what I saw
She came to the bar looking for a man that
Would look pass her mess; with one thing
On his mind and that's to get under her dress

So, ladies check this out and keep this in mind
Many men out here are just like me. We're looking
For the total package, not just a good time and a freebie

Whips and Chains

Traveling back in time, they were enrobed
In chains as they were forced
Onto creaking ships packed together like sardines, scared and
Confused and biting their trembling lips
Some endured but many died
Under the brutal whip

Moving forward to a different time of riots and walks, great men
Had talks about changing the nation; but the whips and
Chains hit their backs and bound their feet, while men
Rode on horses under a sheet; yet one great
Woman still refused to give up her seat

We strive today to break the whips and chains that left deep
Seated memories of fire bombs and dog attacks

The whips and chains remain around our young men today
Hands up obeying the man, one walks down the street playing
His music moving to the beat; the law rides up and gives
The command, "Get down on the curb and sit on your hands"
But, before he can he becomes another statistic to the man

Shoot to kill, ask questions later; leaves yet another mother
To mourn her dead son. Senseless killings go unchecked it is
A sign of the time, that the whips and chains of yesteryear
Continue to bind our necks and mess with our minds

Cynthia Young

Why Did I Come In Here?

I have things to do, places to go
And people to see, getting ready
To go out really frustrates me

I lose my focus easily going from room
To room trying to remember —
Why did I come in here?

Glasses, keys, cell phone, I
Have to look for these things
Before I can even leave home

Why did I come in here? Is my
New catch phrase; it seems
I say it more and more these days

Losing and misplacing this or that
I refuse to accept that I have a bad case
Of I can't remember s**t

Why did I come in here?
Strikes fear in young and old alike
But I will not give in to my mind
Changing like the wind
I will fight this fickle change all
The way to the end

Womb to the Tomb

From the womb to the tomb, I have been there for you
But there are things you need to do too

When you get grown, you need to stand
On your own two feet
Stop calling me every time you need a ride
It's a damn shame you can't get up on
Bus fare — where is your pride?

From the womb to the tomb
I have been there, but
Baby, get your priorities straight
Pay your rent before you put those tracks
In your hair

Take care of your children
I took care of mine, don't think you're
Going to hog all of my time

I love you all the time, but I
Don't like your nasty frame of mind

Smart talking me and giving me attitude
Really makes me see you have no respect

Momma is tired and needs a break; trust and believe me
Taking care of grown ass children is not going to be my fate

You are not the person I yearned for you to be
So I am giving you some room; because I can not
Let your crap send me to the tomb

Cynthia Young

Woodward Avenue

From the Boulevard to Mack – Woodward was the main track
Men approached women talking plenty of smack
Propositions and promises are made and money
Is flowing to break luck

This stroll was busy with women of all types
Big or small curvy or not, these women
Dressed in clothes to make a man hot

Here comes the Big Four, chasing them down
Women scattered an ran all around
They ran down dark alleys, hid in doorways and
Behind parked cars, trying to keep
From scraping their knees and making scars

Pimp's in Cadillac's showed up to save their girls
From a trip to 1300 Beaubien
A trip to jail, would stop their money from flowing

Back on the track the very next night, the women
Let it all hang out, holding nothing back

This is the life they lead on the track
It's just another night as they begin their trek
Down Woodward - from the Boulevard to Mack

CYNTHOLOGY
A Collection of Rhymes

Book I

READER FAVORITES

Broken Moon

A Broken Moon
In
Midnight skies brings
Salty tears to my eyes
It reflects the way I feel

My head and heart still reel
From a heavy loss that rocked
My world

My mother went to sleep
And
Quietly left this world
Leaving behind her little girl

A Broken Moon comes and goes
Like my salty tears that
Ebb and flow

Perhaps one day soon
I'll look differently
At the
Broken Moon,
But not just yet,
It's still too soon

Dangerous Curves

Dangerous curves from head to toe
This girl was fabulous when she walked out the door

Men wanted her to be their wife
Showered her with
Mink coats and diamond rings
These are just a few of the gifts they bring

They look and they wonder what it would be like
To ride her dangerous curves all through the night

Ahh, those curves make men and women swoon
With thoughts that make them howl
Like a wolf at the moon

She walks with her head held high
Never seeming to notice the commotion she caused

She walks with purpose and grace
Then suddenly turns and nods to her admirers
With a beautiful smile on her face

Detroit

Detroit, I love your
Motown sound

I was a kid in the 60's when I heard
The Temptations,
Marvin Gaye and the Four Tops
For the first time

Mustangs, Cadillac's, Electra 225
The big three auto makers
Pumped out the coolest rides

Belle Isle and the Bob Lo Boat
Bring lots of good memories
To mind

We danced at the Graystone
And
The 20 Grand
Listening to all our favorite bands

Lions and Tigers, cheered on by fans
Big D baseball caps
Can be seen on most any man

Through riots and fires
You still struggle for life
Neighborhoods tell a sad story of strife

My home town still has plenty of pride
Stand up big D
And
Come back to life!

Cynthia Young

Fluid Hips

Fluid hips can make a man lick his lips
She sways and gyrates back and forth, leaving
Him swooning as she leaves the dance floor
The crowd yelled to come back and give them more

He speaks slick words to get her alone
As he walks with her arm and arm
On her way home

She knows his kind, she's too smart to
Let him get in her mind

She smiled at him as she slipped away
As he looked at her with longing in his eyes
He tried to conceal the swelling that
Crept between his thighs

Her fluid hips, were tempting
He wanted to fill her with his seed
But he'd have to keep licking his lips
With his hand in his pocket dreaming
About doing the deed

Get Some Business of Your Own

The break up was fresh, tears flowed and flowed
Then anger set in and you had to talk with your girls
Rage and revenge set in, it was all you could think of

But wise and cool your best friend took you to school
She said girl don't you fret, dry those tears
You've got a lot going for you, don't
Worry about what he's doing
Get some business of your own
And watch how fast his ass wants to come back home

Stop watching and calling and crying the blues
Get some business of your own
And he'll be the one pursuing you

Don't have any regrets, things happen for a reason
Men come and go for a lifetime or a season
If he's meant for you, he'll come back
And straighten up his act

Meanwhile, get some business of your own
And there is no doubt he'll drop that other woman
When he finds out that the grass wasn't greener like he thought

Cynthia Young

High Heel Shoes

Now let me tell you about high heel shoes
You know how much they give our feet the blues

But, Baby you know how to strut your stuff
When you wear those sexy high heel shoes

There's no time to worry about corns on your feet
Show off your pretty legs as you sway down the street

Short skirts, pants and the like; don't have
Much flavor without that six inch spike!

So go on girl, give the high heel shoes a whirl
And rock your man's sexy world

There's no time to snooze 'cause he'll be peeping at you
While you slip out of your bad ass high heel shoes

He'll take off your clothes and slide down your hose
You'll love it when he's rubbing your feet
'Cause he ain't planning on letting you sleep

I Don't Want To

Can you do this, will you do that
No, I don't want to

Words I don't often say, but need to
To learn to survive day to day

People are all over me, do this, do that
Can't you see, I don't have any time
Left for me
So,
No, I don't want to

Leave me alone, I just want to listen to
This song, take a long hot bath
Watch my favorite TV show and laugh

Pay this bill, go here, and go there
Sometimes I want to pull out my hair
Don't ask me again
Because, what?
I don't want to

I get it, you're needy and kind' a greedy
Hogging all my time, not leaving
Me space to have my peace of mind
I'll tell you again
And
Yes, I'm still your friend, momma and wife
But
I don't want to….

Seriously, you need to get a life!

No Prospects

Talking on the phone with my girl,
And she tells me, things aren't all that cool
In her world

Too many things not going her way
No money, no man, no prospects today

She says she's cool, 'cause the last thing
She needs, is some broke down tool

With no money, no job, no car and up to no good
Who wants to be with someone
Acting like a hood

She's content to be alone,
So there'll be no
Rejects up in her home

Instead of being with a dead head
There's something to be said
About being alone in bed

Do what you got to do, use
Your toys to bring you joy

She swears, she's not worried and there's no hurry
No prospects now, doesn't **_mean_** ..... She
Won't **_eventually,_** get the man of her dreams

Sagging Pants

Pants baggy and sagging, running from the po po
Hiding behind garbage cans, hoping and praying
I can out run the man

My pants are falling down and so am I
The man is hooking me up, I'm on
My way to the can
All because of my sagging pants

My momma said this would happen to me
She wanted me to be all I can be
Now I'm headed to a cell
I feel like I'm in hell
All because of my sagging pants

Showing my under wear and the crack of my ass
Now, I'm running from some muscle bound broth' a
Lord help me, where is my mother

Trying to look like something I'm not
Don't worry Momma, I'm not going
To jail to rot

No more running from the man
I'm pulling up my sagging pants
These streets are too mean for me
I'm ready to be all I can be

Sons and Daughters

Son's and daughter's take heed
You are a product from our seed
You're the new generation
To take over this great nation

We've laid the ground work but
There is still much to do
To save this country and the world
From prejudice, slavery and injustice too

Hold your head up and step to the plate
We know you can be great, be responsible
It's never too late

Young men, pick up your pants
How in the world can you even dance
Young ladies, classy is the impression
You want to leave, not slutty
Wearing a whacked weave

Facebook, Twitter and the like
Be careful what you post there
It can be seen by anyone, anywhere

Keep your heads on straight and make
Us proud, you are the future
We'll say it loud
You are the future, make us proud!

Touch Me

Touch me, I know you want to
Touch me, I want you to
Slide your hand down
And touch the crown

Touch me, it's what you've been waiting for
I want you to touch deep down in the groove
Don't worry, I won't move

Sensual and hot, your breath on me makes
Me tingle and I visualize the motion of the sea
Rocking deep down inside of me

Your touch is velvet, I love it so
Don't stop stroking me, 'til I say
You can go....come on and touch me

Velvet Lips

Velvet Lips, soft and pink loves him
In all of his glory, so I'll keep the
Secret, and I won't go deep
Into his story

Velvet Lips, soft and pink
Makes him stop to think
How will he kiss those lips to
Bring his juices to their tip

Velvet Lips, soft and pink, quivers and
Sighs deep down inside, bringing great joy and
Tears to a grown man's eyes

He strokes those Velvet Lips, softly and
Kisses them often and those images are
Fresh in his head when he wakes
Up feeling lucky that she is in his bed

Legacy

I want to leave a legacy behind and
Tell the story I acquired over time

A story that can only be mine
Is my legacy to leave behind

I leave memories of my past, for my
Daughter to see and
I pray she will be proud of me

I leave a trail of love for my husband
Who stuck with me

I leave love letters for my mom and dad

I leave laughter and joy for my true friends that
Loved and supported me through thick and thin

This book is my legacy for all to know
I lived life to the fullest and I want to
Show, that it wasn't for nothing and
I will live on, in my rhymes and books
To a back drop of my favorite songs

About the Author

Photograph by Darryl Young
Hairstyle by Kim Best

Cynthia Young was born and raised in Detroit, Michigan. She graduated from Northwestern High School and later moved to California, where she resides with her husband. In 2006 she retired from her career as a human resources consultant in the aerospace industry. She enjoys interior design and martial arts. Young continues to evolve as an author and is already working on her next book.

After many years of caring for the elders in her family, Young wrote her second book *Cynthology A Collection of Rhymes*. She used her rhymes as a way to decompress and express her views on various subjects that are relevant in today's society. It is the first book in the Cynthology collection and includes one hundred unedited original rhymes. She wrote them to be relatable to readers from 18 to 80.

Memoirs of a Caregiver is Young's first book. She shares her journey of twelve years caring for her mother, two aunts and a cousin. All of them suffered from Alzheimer's disease and each of them lived alone in Detroit, requiring Young to travel there during these years to care for them. The long distance complicated her care efforts and trial and error taught her many things.

While telling her poignant story she shares what she learned throughout these years. She guides you on how to become a court appointed conservator and guardian, attend court hearings without an attorney, file court documents, how to research the internet for housing and funding, and much more.

A portion of the proceeds from Memoirs of a Caregiver is donated to the Alzheimer's Association.

Printed in the United States
By Bookmasters